Anthony Curcis's

soccer WORLD ALL-STARS

LaLiga Legends

THIS BOOK BELONGS TO:

_____

Anthony Curcio's

soccer WORLD ALL-STARS

PLAYERS

of goals scored

# of games played   # of assists made

2018-19 season stats

G	GLS	AST
30	12	11

years as player → CAREER
2005-Present

G	GLS	AST
358	76	124

Career totals

ALEXIS SÁNCHEZ
#7^M

2018-19 season stats

G	GLS	AST
20	1	3

CAREER
2008-Present

G	GLS	AST
340	123	64

ANDRÉS
INIESTA
#6^M

2018-19 season stats

G	GLS	AST
14	3	3

CAREER
2002-Present

G	GLS	AST
478	44	74

ÁNGEL
DÍ MARÍA
#11ᴹ

2018-19 season stats		
G	GLS	AST
30	12	11

CAREER
2005-Present

G	GLS	AST
358	76	124

4

#7F

ANTOINE
GREIZMANN

2018-19 season stats		
G	GLS	AST
37	15	8

CAREER 2009-Present		
G	GLS	AST
371	144	50

5

ARJEN ROBBEN #10^M

2018-19 season stats

G	GLS	AST
12	4	0

CAREER
2000-2019

G	GLS	AST
420	150	98

#31ᴹ
BASTIAN
SCHWEINSTEIGER

2018-19 season stats		
G	GLS	AST
31	4	5

CAREER
2002-Present

G	GLS	AST
445	54	68

#7[F]

CRISTIANO RONALDO

2018-19 season stats

G	GLS	AST
31	21	8

CAREER

2002-Present

G	GLS	AST
554	424	141

EDEN
HAZARD
#10ᴹ

2018-19 season stats

G	GLS	AST
37	16	15

CAREER
2007-Present

G	GLS	AST
399	122	86

FRANCK RIBÉRY
#7ᴹ

2018-19 season stats		
G	GLS	AST
25	6	3

CAREER
2004-Present

G	GLS	AST
376	100	118

GARETH
BALE
#11ᴹ

2018-19 season stats

G	GLS	AST
29	8	3

CAREER
2005-Present

G	GLS	AST
347	128	72

adidas

Fly
Emirates

2018-19 season stats

G	GLS	AST
20	7	3

CAREER
2008-Present

G	GLS	AST
226	77	81

LIONEL
MESSI
#10 F

2018-19 season stats

G	GLS	AST
34	36	13

CAREER
2004-Present

G	GLS	AST
458	427	167

LUIS SUÁREZ
#9ᶠ

2018-19 season stats

G	GLS	AST
33	21	6

CAREER
2006-Present

G	GLS	AST
422	296	130

14

MANUEL NEUER
#1ᴳ

2018-19 SEASON STATS

GS	SV	FS
50	90	5

GOALIE

MARCO REUS
#11F

2018-19 season stats

G	GLS	AST
27	17	8

CAREER
2008-Present

G	GLS	AST
298	125	61

EVONIK

MESUT ÖZIL

#10^{M}

2018-19 season stats

G	GLS	AST
24	5	2

CAREER
2006-Present

G	GLS	AST
375	64	128

17

NEYMAR
#10 F

2018-19 season stats

G	GLS	AST
17	15	7

CAREER
2009-Present

G	GLS	AST
165	106	58

18

PAUL
POGBA
#6^M

2018-19 season stats

G	GLS	AST
35	13	9

CAREER
2011-Present

G	GLS	AST
224	52	48

adidas

CHEVROLET

ROBERT LEWANDOWSKI
#9 F

2018-19 season stats

G	GLS	AST
33	22	7

CAREER
2008-2020

G	GLS	AST
359	250	49

ZLATAN
IBRAHIMOVIĆ
#9 F

SERGIO AGÜERO
#10 F

2018-19 season stats

G	GLS	AST
33	21	8

CAREER
2002-Present

G	GLS	AST
425	248	71

SERGIO RAMOS

#4^D

2018-19 season stats

G	GLS	AST
28	6	1

CAREER
2003-Present

G	GLS	AST
470	63	26

THIAGO SILVA #2^D

Fly Emirates

2018-19 season stats

G	GLS	AST
25	0	1

CAREER
2004-Present

G	GLS	AST
287	14	5

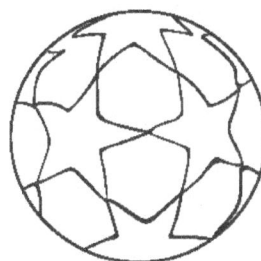

24

THOMAS MÜLLER

#25 M/F

2018-19 season stats

G	GLS	AST
32	6	9

CAREER
2008-Present

G	GLS	AST
329	110	101

Messi

10

Messi

10

Ronaldo

7

Ronaldo

7

Neymar

10

LaLiga Legends

Biography

Biography

XAVI #6 M
HERNÁNDEZ

CAREER
1999-2015

G	GLS	AST
488	57	105

Xavier Hernandez was born January 25, 1980 in Barcelona, Spain. "Xavi" joined F.C. Barcelona's "La Masia" youth system when he was only 11 years old. Xavi's dad was a former player who played in the first division for Sabadell. Many soccer fans consider Xavi to be one of the best, if not, the best central midfielder's of all-time. He was known for finding gaps in the defense and exploiting them. "That's what I do: look for spaces. All day. I'm always looking." Xavi said. He would find that space, receive a pass from a teammate and move the ball quickly upfield. Xavi was a great team player, who played his position perfectly. Xavi twice led the La Liga in assists, and consistently was in the top 10 in both assists and goals.

Biography

RONALDO
#9 F

Ronaldo Luis Nazario de Lima, aka and commonly known simply as "Ronaldo" is a soccer superstar from Brazil, who played as a striker. His nickname was "The Phenomenon", and he is widely considered one of the greatest soccer players of all time. Ronaldo had amazing dribbling speed and could cover a lot of ground very quickly. By the age of 23, Ronaldo had scored over 200 goals for club and country. Had it not been for knee injuries, his career statistics would have continued into superstar status. Ronaldo was born in Rio De Janeiro, Brazil on September 18, 1976. Ronaldo won the FIFA World Player of the Year award in 1996, 1997 and 2002!

34

Biography

#10 M/F
DIEGO
MARADONA

CAREER
1976-1997

G	GLS	AST
590	310	N/A

Diego Maradona, born 1960 in Argentina, is regarded by fans, sports writers, and players alike to be one of the greatest soccer players of all time. Maradona measures at 5'5", which gives him a low center of gravity - useful for maneuvering around other players. Because of his unexpected speed, Maradona was often singled out by the opposing teams, earning the nickname, "The Golden Boy." Maradona played for Argentinos Juniors, Boca Juniors, Barcelona, Napoli, Sevilla, Newell's Old Boys, and then returned to Boca Juniors. He played nationally for Argentina U20 (for players under 20 years old) and Argentina. In 1986, Argentina won victory over West Germany in the World Cup, with The Golden Boy as their captain... South American Player of the Year, best Argentine sportsman of the year, won FIFA's Golden Ball as best soccer player of the year, Spanish King's Cup Champion, World Champion with Argentina, FIFA Player of the Century (shared with Pelé)... The awards keep going!

Biography

FRANZ
BECKENBAUER

#5 D

CAREER
1963-1983

G	GLS	AST
709	94	N/A

Franz Beckenbauer, born 1945, is a former German soccer star. Nicknamed "The Emperor" because of his elegance on his feet, Beckenbauer is widely regarded on of the best player in soccer history. Beckenbauer played for over 10 years for Bayern Munich, then played for the New York Cosmos, Hamburger SV, and went back to end his playing career with Cosmos... Beckenbauer played nationally for West Germany 1965-1977. U.S. National Soccer Hall of Fame, West German soccer player of the year, won Bundesliga and German Cup titles, defeated Holland 2-1 to win the 1974 World Cup title, North American Soccer League MVP... An impressive career!

JOHAN CRUYFF
#14 M/F

CAREER
1957-1984

G	GLS	AST
514	290	N/A

Johan Cruyff, born 1947 in the Netherlands, is a former Dutch soccer star player and coach. Born on a street just five minutes away from Ajax's Stadium (where his champion career would begin), Cruyff was destined to be a star. Cruyff started his soccer career with Ajax at the age of 10 and played for them for 16 year, advancing in league. He then played for Barcelona, the Los Angeles Aztecs, the Washington Diplomats, Levante, Ajax once again, and ended his playing career with Feyenoord, while playing nationally for the Netherlands 1966-1977... Ballon d'Or Award, European Golden Shoe, Dutch Footballer (Soccer Player) of the Year, Sportsman of the Year... An outstanding player!

Biography

MANÉ GARRINCHA

#7ᵂ

CAREER
1951-1972

G	GLS	AST
345	102	N/A

Mané Garrincha, born 1933 in Brazil, is known as one of the greatest dribblers of all time. As the first player to the win Golden Ball (Player of the Tournament), Golden Boot (Leading Goalscorer), and the World Cup all in the same tournament, no one could argue Garrincha's talent. Players had never encountered a winger who could beat them with such ease - let alone one who was bowlegged. Garrincha had two nicknames - Anjo de Pernas Tortas (Bent-Legged Angel) and Alegria do Povo (People's Joy). The people of Brazil loved him. Starting his senior career with Serrano, Garrincha also played for Botafogo, Brazil, Corinthians, Atlético Junior, Flamengo, and Olaria. Garrincha played nationally for Brazil 1955-1966... 2x World Cup Champion, 3x O'Higgins Cup winner, World Cup Golden Ball and Golden Boot Awards, Ballon d'Or Award, named to World Soccer's Greatest Players of the 20th Century!

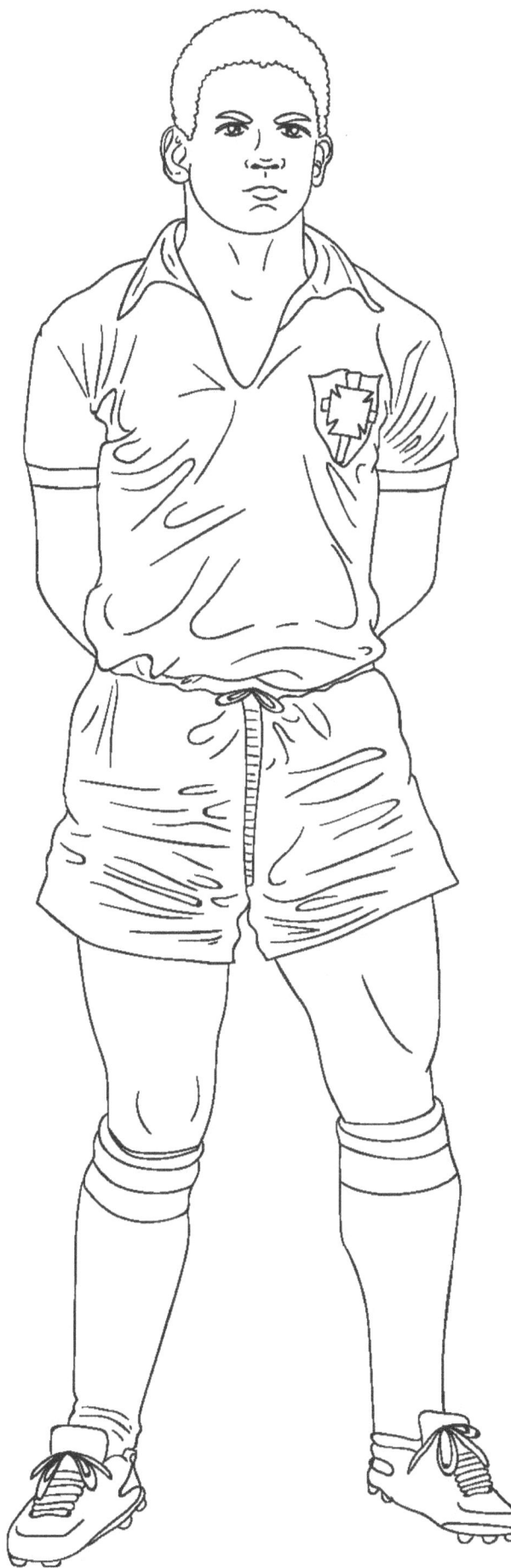

MARCO VAN BASTEN

#9 F

CAREER
1981-1995

G	GLS	AST
373	277	N/A

Marco van Basten, born 1964 in the Netherlands, was the best of the best. In his high profile career that ended at the young age of 28, Van Basten scored 300 goals. Van Basten played for Ajax, Milan, Netherlands U21 (National - under 21 years old), and the Netherlands (National). He was known for his close ball control, attacking intelligence, elegant headers, and unprecedented strikes and volleys! ... Ballon d'Or Award, FIFA World Player of the Year, European Cup Top Scorer, European Golden Boot, World Soccer Player of the Year, Italian Football (Soccer) Hall of Fame, A.C. Milan Hall of Fame... And many more accomplishments!

PAOLO MALDINI #3^D

PAOLO **MALDINI** #3ᴰ

CAREER
1984-2009

G	GLS	AST
902	33	N/A

Paolo Maldini, born 1968 in Milan, is known as one of the greatest defenders of all time. Maldini played at a world-class level for the entirety of his career, which spanned more than two decades. Maldini spent all 25 years of his Serie A career with A.C. Milan. Maldini played nationally of Italy U21 (Italy - under 21 years old) and Italy from 1988-2002... FIFA World Cup All-Star Team, World Soccer Player of the Year, Most appearances in all competitions with 902 (A.C. Milan), Most FIFA World Cup appearances for Italy (23)... Impressive career!

ZINEDINE ZIDANE #10 M

CAREER
1988-2006

G	GLS	AST
684	125	N/A

Zinedine Zidane, nicknamed Zizou, was born in France in 1972. Zidane was a star of the sport, known for his elite playmaking ability, elegance, vision, ball-control, and technique. Zidane spent his senior career with Cannes, Bordeaux, Juventus, and Real Madrid. He played nationally for France U17, France U18, France U21, and France (1994-2006). Zidane is currently a team manager for Real Madrid... FIFA World Cup (1998) and World Cup Runner-Up (2006), French Division 1 Player of the Year, Ballon d'Or Award, FIFA World Player of the Year, Fox Sports Player of the Decade, ESPN Team of the Decade, FIFA World Player of the Year, FIFA World Cup Golden Ball... The list keeps going!

Biography

RONALDINHO
GAÚCHO
#10 M

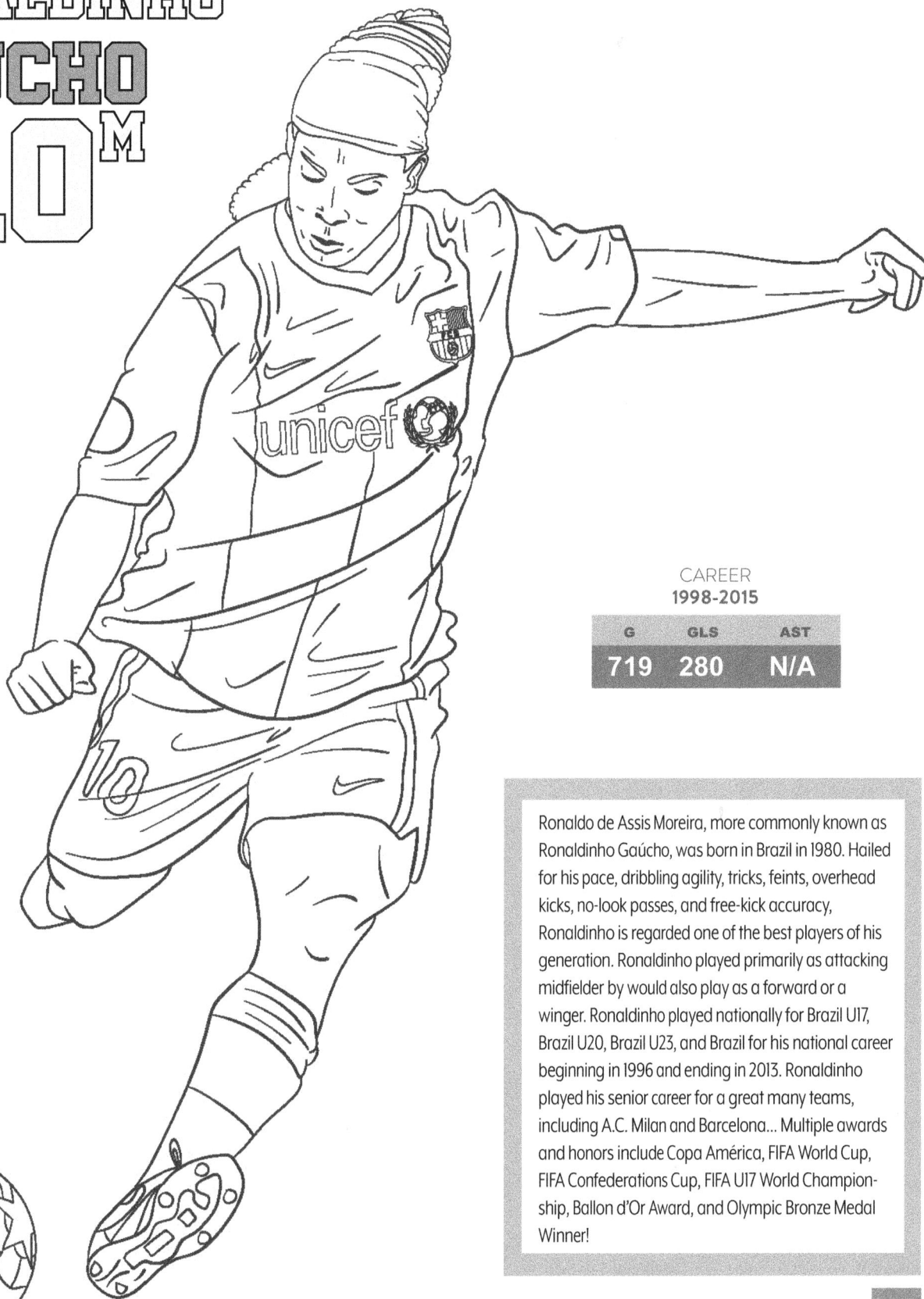

CAREER
1998-2015

G	GLS	AST
719	280	N/A

Ronaldo de Assis Moreira, more commonly known as Ronaldinho Gaúcho, was born in Brazil in 1980. Hailed for his pace, dribbling agility, tricks, feints, overhead kicks, no-look passes, and free-kick accuracy, Ronaldinho is regarded one of the best players of his generation. Ronaldinho played primarily as attacking midfielder by would also play as a forward or a winger. Ronaldinho played nationally for Brazil U17, Brazil U20, Brazil U23, and Brazil for his national career beginning in 1996 and ending in 2013. Ronaldinho played his senior career for a great many teams, including A.C. Milan and Barcelona... Multiple awards and honors include Copa América, FIFA World Cup, FIFA Confederations Cup, FIFA U17 World Championship, Ballon d'Or Award, and Olympic Bronze Medal Winner!

PELE

#10 F/M

CAREER
1956-1977

G	GLS	AST
812	757	N/A

Edson Arantes do Nascimento, known as Pelé, was born in 1940 in Brazil. Pelé is regarded by most as the greatest soccer player of all time. Pelé began playing at the young age of 16 for the Brazil national team and averaged a goal per game throughout his entire career. In Brazil, Pelé is praised as national hero not only for his stardom on the field and record-breaking achievements, but also for his humanitarian efforts. Pelé played his senior career for Santos and the New York Cosmos and played nationally for Brazil 1957-1971. FIFA World Cup Best Young Player, FIFA World Cup Golden Ball (Best Player), South American Championship Best Player and Top Scorer, FIFA Order of Merit, FIFA Centennial Award, FIFA Player of the Century (shared with Diego Maradona)... Additionally, Pelé was elected Citizen of the World by the U.N. and elected Goodwill Ambassador by UNESCO!

43

soccer WORLD ALL-STARS

Extras

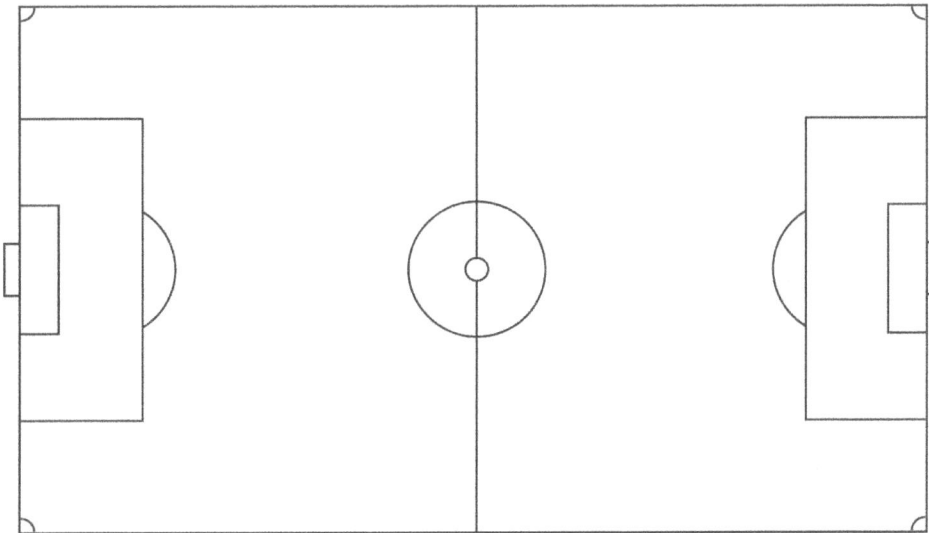

Design YOUR team uniform

Design YOUR team uniform

ATHLETIC CLUB
X X
BILBAO

VALENCIA C. de F.

1889

GETAFE C.F.S.A.D.

CRISTIANO
RONALDO

www.ingramcontent.com/pod-product-compliance
Lightning Source LLC
Chambersburg PA
CBHW081217020426
42331CB00012B/3039